Cryptocurrency Simplified

From Bitcoin to DeFi for Money Making

Abdullahi YUSUF

Table of Contents:

INTRODUCTION4

Brief introduction of the purpose of the book and the importance of cryptocurrency.   4

CHAPTER 1: UNDERSTANDING THE BASICS6

Define cryptocurrency.   6
Historical context: The origin of cryptocurrencies.   9
How cryptocurrencies work: Blockchain technology.   11
Different types of cryptocurrencies (Bitcoin, Ethereum, and others).   14

CHAPTER 2: BUYING AND STORING CRYPTOCURRENCY17

How to buy cryptocurrencies. 17
Cryptocurrency exchanges and wallets. 19
Cold storage vs. hot storage. 22

CHAPTER 3: INVESTING AND TRADING24

Investment strategies in cryptocurrencies.   24
Day trading vs. HODLing.   25
Risks and rewards.   25

CHAPTER 4: MINING AND STAKING27

What is mining and how it works. 27
Staking and earning passive income. 28
The environmental impact of mining. 29

CHAPTER 5: INITIAL COIN OFFERINGS (ICOS) AND TOKENS31

What are ICOs? 31
The rise and fall of ICOs. 32
Utility tokens vs. security tokens. 33

CHAPTER 6: SECURITY AND RISKS34

Common security threats (hacks, scams, phishing).   34
How to protect your investments.   35
Two-factor authentication and hardware wallets.   35

CHAPTER 7: REGULATION AND LEGAL FRAMEWORK37

Cryptocurrency regulation by country.   37
Anti-money laundering (AML) and Know Your Customer (KYC) laws.   38
The role of government and regulatory bodies.   38

CHAPTER 8: ALTCOINS AND TOKENS40

An overview of various altcoins and tokens.　　40
Prominent projects and their use cases.　　42
Diversifying your portfolio.　　45

CHAPTER 9: DECENTRALIZED FINANCE (DEFI)49

What is DeFi?   49
Key Defi applications   51
Risks and opportunities in DeFi.   53

CHAPTER 10: THE FUTURE OF CRYPTOCURRENCY55

Emerging technologies (NFTs, smart contracts).	55
Scaling solutions (Layer 2, sharding).	58
Predictions for the future of cryptocurrencies.	60

CHAPTER 11: TAXES AND REPORTING64

Tax implications of cryptocurrency transactions.   64
Reporting requirements.   65
Working with tax professionals.   65

CHAPTER 12: TOKENOMICS AND TOKEN SALES67

What is Tokenomics. 67
Token Distribution. 67
Token Utility. 68
Token Burning 68
The Role of Tokenomics in Project Success 68

CONCLUSION 69

Summary of key takeaways. 69
Encouraging responsible investment and continued learning. 70

Appendix: Additional Resources 72
Useful websites, tools, and services for cryptocurrency enthusiasts.

INTRODUCTION: THE DIGITAL REVOLUTION - UNVEILING CRYPTOCURRENCY'S SECRETS

In a world defined by rapid technological progress and a constant thirst for innovation, few concepts have captivated our collective imagination quite like cryptocurrency. This revolutionary form of digital currency has transcended the bounds of traditional finance, spawning a financial ecosystem that promises to reshape the way we conduct transactions, invest, and interact with the digital world.

The purpose of this book is to provide you with an enlightening journey through the realms of cryptocurrency. As the title suggests, "Cryptocurrency Simplified: From Bitcoin to DeFi for Money Making," our goal is to offer you a comprehensive understanding of what cryptocurrency is, how it works, and why it matters in making money in today's world.

The importance of cryptocurrency cannot be overstated. Beyond its role as a digital medium of exchange, it embodies the principles of decentralization, security, and financial empowerment. By delving deep into the mysteries and intricacies of cryptocurrencies, you'll be better equipped to harness their potential, make informed decisions, and participate in a financial landscape that is both thrilling and transformative.

In the chapters that follow, we will navigate through the fundamental concepts of cryptocurrencies, from their historical roots to the latest developments in this dynamic field. You will discover how to buy, store, and invest in cryptocurrencies, all while staying safe from the ever-present threats that lurk in the digital shadows. We'll explore the various types of cryptocurrencies, the rise and fall of Initial Coin Offerings (ICOs), the fascinating world of decentralized finance (DeFi), and so much more.

As we embark on this journey together, keep in mind that the cryptocurrency space is constantly evolving. New technologies, regulations, and innovations emerge at a remarkable pace. Our aim is not only to provide you with a snapshot of the cryptocurrency landscape at this moment but also to equip you with the knowledge and tools to stay informed and adapt to the ever-changing environment.

So, whether you're a novice intrigued by the idea of cryptocurrency, an investor looking to diversify your portfolio or someone simply curious about the digital revolution, this book is designed to be your compass through the world of cryptocurrency. It's an invitation to explore the uncharted territories of digital finance, unlocking the secrets and opportunities that this exciting realm holds.

Let's embark on this journey together, starting with the fundamentals, and venture deeper into the world of cryptocurrency, discovering its vast potential, risks, and rewards.

1.0. CHAPTER 1: UNDERSTANDING THE BASICS

1.1. **Define Cryptocurrency**: Cryptocurrency is a revolutionary form of digital or virtual currency that uses cryptography for security. Unlike traditional currencies issued by governments, such as the US dollar or the euro, cryptocurrencies are decentralized and typically operate on a technology called blockchain. The core characteristics of cryptocurrencies include:

1.1.1 Decentralization: A Paradigm Shift

The hallmark feature of cryptocurrency is its profound departure from traditional centralized financial systems. In a world where governments and financial institutions traditionally issue and regulate currencies, cryptocurrencies are liberated from such central control. Instead, they thrive within a decentralized framework. This decentralization is the bedrock of the cryptocurrency universe, allowing it to function independently and free from the constraints of a single governing entity. Decentralization is achieved through a distributed ledger, a monumental innovation underpinning cryptocurrencies. In this context, a distributed ledger means that transaction data is not confined to a central repository but is instead duplicated across a network of participants. These participants are akin to the guardians of the cryptocurrency ecosystem, often referred to as miners or validators. Miners and validators play a pivotal role in maintaining the integrity of the system. They verify and record transactions, ensuring that all participants in the network have consensus on the state of the ledger. This process, accomplished through cryptographic techniques, establishes trust without the need for a central authority. In essence, the trust is decentralized and shared across the network. This feature has far-reaching implications, including resistance to censorship, increased security, and the elimination of single points of failure.

1.1.2 Digital Nature: Beyond Physical Borders

Unlike the physical coins and paper bills that we are accustomed to, cryptocurrencies are purely digital entities. They exist exclusively as strings of code and data within the blockchain. This digital nature brings about a range of benefits and innovations. Digital currencies transcend the constraints of physical geography. They are not bound by national borders or the limitations of physical transportation. In a world where we can instantaneously communicate with anyone globally, the digital nature of cryptocurrencies aligns perfectly with the demands of a modern, interconnected world. Regardless of where you are on the planet, as long as you have an internet connection, you can seamlessly participate in the world of cryptocurrencies.

Furthermore, the digital nature of cryptocurrencies allows for ease of use in the digital realm. Online transactions, digital wallets, and peer-to-peer exchanges all become possible due to this purely digital existence.

1.1.3 Cryptography: The Shield of Security

Security lies at the core of cryptocurrencies, and it is the cryptographic techniques employed that provide this essential safeguard. Cryptography, the science of encoding and decoding information, serves as a formidable shield, protecting the integrity and privacy of cryptocurrency transactions. Complex mathematical algorithms, known as cryptographic hash functions, are employed to secure transactions. These algorithms create a unique digital fingerprint for each transaction, making it extremely challenging for unauthorized parties to tamper with or gain access to the transaction details. This security layer ensures that once a transaction is recorded on the blockchain, it is nearly immutable, making it resistant to fraud and tampering.

Cryptography also plays a pivotal role in creating cryptographic addresses, which are used to represent the identities of participants in cryptocurrency transactions. These addresses add a layer of privacy, reducing the reliance on personal information. While this pseudonymity enhances privacy, it's essential to note that it doesn't guarantee complete anonymity. Cryptocurrency transactions are still recorded on a public ledger, which leads to a level of transparency that can be both empowering and potentially revealing. This amalgamation of security measures, combined with the distributed and decentralized nature of cryptocurrencies, contributes to their resilience against fraud, theft, and unauthorized access, adding an additional layer of trust to the ecosystem.

1.1.4 Global Accessibility: Uniting the World

The global accessibility of cryptocurrencies stands as a testament to their inclusivity. Unlike traditional financial systems, which often come with restrictions and exclusions based on geographical locations and socioeconomic factors, cryptocurrencies are a financial frontier that knows no geographical boundaries. Whether you reside in a bustling metropolis or a remote village, as long as you have access to the internet, you can participate in the cryptocurrency ecosystem. This inclusivity empowers individuals who have been previously excluded from the traditional financial system, allowing them to engage in economic activities, investment opportunities, and cross-border transactions.

This global accessibility not only reshapes financial inclusion but also has implications for remittances, international trade, and cross-border collaborations. Cryptocurrencies have the potential to bridge financial gaps, offering solutions to individuals and communities that have previously faced financial isolation.

1.1.5   Pseudonymity: Balancing Privacy and Transparency

In the cryptocurrency realm, transactions are recorded on the blockchain, and the participants are often represented by cryptographic addresses rather than their real-world identities. This pseudonymity provides a level of privacy and anonymity, enhancing the security of participants' personal information. However, it's crucial to understand that pseudonymity is not synonymous with complete anonymity. While transactions are recorded on a public ledger, the identities behind the cryptographic addresses are often difficult to discern. This balance between privacy and transparency allows individuals to protect their personal information while ensuring the integrity of the network. Pseudonymity also aligns with the principles of decentralization and trust. It empowers individuals to participate in the cryptocurrency ecosystem without revealing their full identities. This can be particularly valuable in regions where privacy concerns or security risks are prevalent. In essence, the pseudonymity of cryptocurrency transactions contributes to the security and privacy of the ecosystem, making it more accessible and secure for a diverse range of participants.

By grasping these fundamental elements, you've taken the first step in unraveling the intricacies of cryptocurrencies.

As we venture further into this eBook, we will explore additional facets of this dynamic and transformative field, including the historical context, the mechanics of blockchain technology, and the myriad of cryptocurrencies that inhabit this exciting digital landscape.

1.2. HISTORICAL CONTEXT – THE ORIGIN OF CRYPTOCURRENCIES

To fully appreciate the remarkable evolution of cryptocurrencies, it's essential to delve into their historical roots. This concise overview will help us understand how cryptocurrencies emerged and the significant milestones that paved the way for the digital financial revolution.

1.2.1. Pre-Bitcoin Era: Explorations in Digital Currency

Before Bitcoin's groundbreaking emergence, several endeavors to create digital currencies were explored. One notable example is "E-gold," which was introduced in 1996. E-gold represented a digital gold currency, allowing users to hold digital representations of gold and make online transactions backed by these gold reserves. The concept held great promise and attracted a substantial user base. However, E-gold encountered significant challenges related to centralization and regulation, ultimately leading to its demise. Regulatory pressures, including concerns about money laundering and its central authority's ability to freeze accounts, culminated in the closure of the E-gold service in 2009. This experience revealed the limitations of early digital currencies and the necessity for a new approach.

1.2.2. Bitcoin's Genesis: A Paradigm-Shifting Moment

The transformative moment in the history of cryptocurrencies transpired in 2008 when an enigmatic individual or group operating under the pseudonym "Satoshi Nakamoto" published the Bitcoin whitepaper. This pivotal document introduced the world to a groundbreaking concept - a peer-to-peer electronic cash system. The whitepaper outlined a vision for a decentralized digital currency that would function without the need for a central authority. This concept laid the foundation for what we now know as cryptocurrencies.

In January 2009, Bitcoin's network was officially launched with the mining of the "genesis block," denoted as "Block 0." This moment marked the birth of Bitcoin and the beginning of a new era in financial innovation. Bitcoin's core tenets were centered on solving the inherent challenges of earlier digital currencies, chiefly by emphasizing decentralization and utilizing blockchain technology. The introduction of the blockchain, a distributed and immutable ledger that would record all Bitcoin transactions, became the cornerstone of this revolutionary system. Unlike its predecessors, Bitcoin was designed to be resistant to central control, censorship, and manipulation.

The anonymous creator, Satoshi Nakamoto, continued to contribute to the development of the Bitcoin network, collaborating with a growing community of early adopters and developers. Over time, Bitcoin's codebase and ecosystem evolved, expanding its use cases beyond a mere medium of exchange. Today, Bitcoin is widely recognized as "digital gold," serving as a store of value, a medium of exchange, and a hedge against inflation.

1.2.3.   The Crypto Boom: Proliferation of Altcoins

Bitcoin's resounding success set in motion a chain reaction, leading to the creation of thousands of alternative cryptocurrencies, frequently referred to as "altcoins." These digital assets emerged to address specific use cases or technological innovations, offering alternatives and enhancements to Bitcoin's original design. Among the first significant altcoins was "Litecoin," launched in 2011 by Charlie Lee. Litecoin differentiated itself by providing faster confirmation times compared to Bitcoin, making it a more suitable choice for day-to-day transactions. This feature contributed to Litecoin's popularity and marked the inception of a diverse range of digital currencies with unique attributes.

As the cryptocurrency landscape continued to evolve, it diversified into various categories, including privacy coins, stablecoins, utility tokens, and more. Each cryptocurrency brought its own set of innovations, use cases, and communities, contributing to the vibrant and ever-expanding ecosystem that we see today. This historical context illuminates the remarkable journey of cryptocurrencies from their early explorations and challenges to the transformative vision outlined in the Bitcoin whitepaper. As we delve deeper into this eBook, we will explore the practical aspects, technological intricacies, and the diverse range of cryptocurrencies that have shaped this dynamic digital financial landscape.

1.3. HOW CRYPTOCURRENCIES WORK - BLOCKCHAIN TECHNOLOGY

Blockchain technology stands as the cornerstone of most cryptocurrencies, providing the infrastructure that makes these digital assets functional and secure. In this section, we will delve into the mechanics of blockchain technology, which underpins the operation of cryptocurrencies.

1.3.1. **Blocks and Transactions: The Building Blocks of Blockchain**

At the heart of a blockchain lies a chain of "blocks," each housing a collection of transactions. These transactions can take various forms, from simple transfers of cryptocurrency between users to the execution of more complex smart contracts. Let's explore these fundamental components in more detail:

- **Blocks:** Each block is a container that holds a set of transactions. These transactions are bundled together into a block before they are added to the blockchain. A block typically includes a reference to the previous block in the chain, creating a chronological order of transactions.
- **Transactions:** These are the actions that users perform with cryptocurrencies. Transactions can include the

transfer of cryptocurrency from one user to another, the execution of a smart contract, or other interactions within the blockchain network. Each transaction contains information about the sender, recipient, the amount being transferred, and a unique digital signature that validates the transaction's authenticity.

1.3.2. Decentralization: The Pillar of Trust

Decentralization is a pivotal concept in the world of blockchain technology. It forms the basis of a blockchain's operation and is crucial for ensuring security, transparency, and resilience. Unlike centralized systems, where a single entity has control, blockchain data is distributed across a network of nodes. These nodes are typically maintained by various participants in the network, such as miners, validators, or full node operators.

The decentralized structure ensures that no single entity or authority holds absolute power over the blockchain. Instead, the collective agreement and validation of transactions are achieved through a consensus mechanism, involving a network of nodes working together. This distributed nature of the blockchain significantly enhances security, making it exceedingly difficult for any single party to manipulate the system. Additionally, it eliminates single points of failure, as there's no central authority to target or compromise.

1.3.3. Consensus Mechanisms: Validating and Securing the Blockchain

The blockchain's integrity and security depend on consensus mechanisms, which are the protocols used to validate and add new blocks to the blockchain. These mechanisms ensure that all participants in the network agree on the state of the ledger. The two most common consensus mechanisms are:

- **Proof of Work (PoW):** This mechanism, employed by Bitcoin and several other cryptocurrencies, involves miners competing to solve complex mathematical puzzles. The first miner to solve the puzzle gets the privilege of adding the next block to the blockchain and is rewarded with cryptocurrency. PoW is known for its energy-intensive nature but is highly effective in securing the network.

- **Proof of Stake (PoS):** An alternative to PoW, PoS is gaining popularity due to its energy efficiency. In PoS, validators are chosen to create new blocks based on the number of cryptocurrency tokens they "stake" or lock up as collateral. This reduces the energy consumption of the network and is employed by cryptocurrencies like Ethereum, which is in the process of transitioning from PoW to PoS.

1.3.4.   Immutable and Transparent: Trust in the Blockchain

Once a transaction is added to the blockchain, it becomes nearly impossible to alter or erase. This immutability ensures the integrity of the transaction history, creating an indelible record. It is this quality that makes the blockchain an ideal ledger for financial transactions and various other applications, such as supply chain tracking and identity verification. Furthermore, blockchain data is typically public and transparent, allowing anyone to verify transactions. This transparency contributes to trust within the system, as users can independently audit the transaction history. While the identities of participants are often represented by cryptographic addresses, their actions within the blockchain are visible for all to see. This combination of immutability and transparency creates a high level of confidence in the accuracy and reliability of blockchain records.

In understanding these foundational principles of blockchain technology, you are well on your way to comprehending the mechanics of cryptocurrencies. As we proceed through this eBook, we will delve deeper into the practical aspects of cryptocurrency, exploring topics such as buying, storing, and investing in digital assets.

1.4. Different Types of Cryptocurrencies - Bitcoin, Ethereum, and Others

Cryptocurrencies form a diverse ecosystem, each designed with unique features and use cases. In this section, we will explore two of the most influential cryptocurrencies, Bitcoin and Ethereum, and then touch upon a variety of other cryptocurrencies, showcasing the breadth and depth of this dynamic digital landscape.

1.4.1. Bitcoin (BTC): The Digital Gold

Bitcoin, often referred to as "digital gold," is the pioneering cryptocurrency and remains the most widely recognized digital asset. Designed by the enigmatic Satoshi Nakamoto, its primary functions are as a store of value and a medium of exchange. Let's delve deeper into its defining characteristics:

- **Store of Value:** Bitcoin's most well-known role is that of a store of value. Similar to gold, it is considered a reliable asset for preserving wealth. Investors often turn to Bitcoin as a hedge against inflation and economic uncertainty, citing its scarcity and its ability to maintain its value over time.
- **Medium of Exchange**: While its primary purpose is as a store of value, Bitcoin is also utilized for cross-border transactions and peer-to-peer payments. Its global accessibility, security, and immutability make it an attractive choice for moving funds across borders or making online purchases.

1.4.2. Ethereum (ETH): The Birth of Smart Contracts

Ethereum introduced groundbreaking innovation to the cryptocurrency space by enabling the execution of smart contracts. These self-executing agreements automatically enforce predefined terms and conditions without the need for intermediaries. This innovation expanded the utility of blockchain technology, leading to the development of decentralized applications (DApps) and decentralized finance (DeFi). Key features of Ethereum include:

- **Smart Contracts:** Ethereum's defining feature is its support for smart contracts. These are computer programs that automatically execute predefined actions when specific conditions are met. Smart contracts have found applications in various industries, including finance, supply chain management, and voting systems.

- **Decentralized Applications (DApps):** Ethereum's platform has facilitated the creation of decentralized applications. DApps are applications that run on a decentralized network of computers, ensuring transparency and security. They have disrupted industries such as gaming, finance, and digital identity.
- **Decentralized Finance (DeFi):** DeFi refers to a set of financial services and applications built on blockchain technology, primarily Ethereum. DeFi platforms offer features like lending, borrowing, trading, and earning interest on cryptocurrencies, all without traditional intermediaries.

1.4.3. The Diversity of Cryptocurrencies: Beyond Bitcoin and Ethereum

Beyond Bitcoin and Ethereum, the cryptocurrency landscape is rich and diverse, with thousands of digital assets, each designed to serve specific purposes. Here are a few notable examples:

- **Monero (XMR):** A privacy-focused cryptocurrency that offers enhanced anonymity and transaction confidentiality. Monero is designed to provide users with a high degree of privacy.

- **Tether (USDT):** A stablecoin that is pegged to the value of a traditional currency, such as the US dollar. Stablecoins offer stability, making them ideal for trading and as a bridge between cryptocurrencies and fiat currencies.
- **Binance Coin (BNB):** A utility token that was originally created for the Binance cryptocurrency exchange. It can be used for various purposes within the Binance ecosystem, including trading fee discounts and participation in token sales.

These examples represent just a fraction of the diverse range of cryptocurrencies available. In the cryptocurrency world, new projects and tokens are constantly emerging, each with its unique features, use cases, and communities.

This chapter has laid a strong foundation for understanding cryptocurrencies, encompassing their fundamental features, historical context, the mechanics of blockchain technology, and an introduction to some of the most prominent cryptocurrencies. As we delve deeper into this book, we will explore practical aspects such as acquiring, securing, and investing in cryptocurrencies, ensuring you are well-prepared to navigate the exciting and evolving world of digital assets.

2.0 CHAPTER 2: BUYING AND STORING CRYPTOCURRENCY

In this chapter, we will explore the practical aspects of buying and storing cryptocurrencies. Understanding how to acquire digital assets and how to securely store them is crucial for anyone entering the world of cryptocurrencies. We will cover the following topics:

2.1 HOW TO BUY CRYPTOCURRENCIES

In this section, we will provide an in-depth guide on how to purchase cryptocurrencies. Buying cryptocurrencies involves several key steps, ensuring that you can successfully convert traditional fiat currency into digital assets. Here's an extensive overview of the process:

- **Step 1: Choose a Cryptocurrency Exchange**

Selecting the right cryptocurrency exchange is the first and crucial step in buying digital assets. It's essential to choose a reputable exchange that aligns with your requirements. Some of the well-known exchanges in the cryptocurrency space include Coinbase, Binance, Kraken, Bitstamp, Bybit and many others. Here are some factors to consider when choosing an exchange:

Security: Assess the exchange's security features, such as two-factor authentication (2FA) and cold storage of funds. You want to ensure your assets are well-protected.

Supported Cryptocurrencies: Verify that the exchange supports the specific cryptocurrency you intend to purchase. Not all exchanges offer the same range of digital assets.

Fees: Be aware of trading fees, withdrawal fees, and other charges. Different exchanges have varying fee structures, and these can significantly affect your overall costs.

User Experience: Evaluate the exchange's user interface and overall user experience. A well-designed platform can make the buying process more straightforward.

- **Step 2: Account Setup**

Once you've chosen an exchange, you need to create an account. Account setup typically involves the following steps:

Registration: Provide your personal information, including your name, email address, and a secure password. You may also need to agree to the exchange's terms and conditions.

Verification: Many exchanges require identity verification to comply with Know Your Customer (KYC) regulations. This process may involve submitting identification documents like a passport or driver's license.

Two-Factor Authentication (2FA): Enable 2FA for your account's security. This adds an extra layer of protection by requiring a verification code from a separate device to access your account.

- **Step 3: Fund Your Account**

After successfully setting up your exchange account, you'll need to deposit traditional currency, such as US dollars or euros, into your account. This can typically be done in various ways:

Bank Transfers: Many exchanges offer the option to deposit funds via bank transfers. You'll be provided with the exchange's bank account details to initiate the transfer.

Credit/Debit Cards: Some exchanges allow users to purchase cryptocurrencies using credit or debit cards. This is a convenient method for quick deposits.

Other Payment Methods: Depending on the exchange, you might have other payment options, including payment processors like PayPal or other cryptocurrencies you already own.

- **Step 4: Place an Order**

With funds in your exchange account, you're ready to place an order for the cryptocurrency you want to buy. There are various order types to choose from:

Market Orders: This type of order is executed immediately at the current market price. Market orders are straightforward and ensure your trade is completed promptly.

Limit Orders: A limit order allows you to specify the price at which you want to buy the cryptocurrency. Your order will only be executed when the market reaches your desired price.

Stop Orders: Stop orders are used to buy a cryptocurrency when it reaches a specific price. This can help you enter a position when the market is moving in your favor.

- **Step 5: Secure Your Assets**

After successfully completing your purchase, it's crucial to transfer your cryptocurrency to a secure wallet for storage. Leaving your assets on the exchange for extended periods can expose them to security risks. The next section will delve into the various types of cryptocurrency wallets and storage methods, ensuring your assets remain safe and under your control.

In the following sections of this chapter, we will further explore cryptocurrency exchanges, wallets, and the critical distinctions between hot and cold storage. Understanding these components will empower you to make informed decisions when buying and securely storing your digital assets.

2.2 **Cryptocurrency Exchanges and Wallets**

Cryptocurrency exchanges serve as the primary entry point for individuals looking to buy, sell, and trade digital assets. They provide a marketplace where users can exchange traditional fiat currency (e.g., US dollars, euros) for cryptocurrencies and vice versa. Here are some key points to consider regarding cryptocurrency exchanges:

- **Variety of Cryptocurrencies**: Exchanges offer a wide range of cryptocurrencies, allowing users to trade major assets like Bitcoin and Ethereum, as well as a plethora of altcoins with varying features and use cases.
- **Trading Pairs**: Cryptocurrency exchanges provide numerous trading pairs, which indicate the cryptocurrencies that can be exchanged for one another. For instance, the Bitcoin/US dollar (BTC/USD) trading pair allows users to trade Bitcoin for US dollars.
- **Liquidity:** Liquidity is crucial for efficient trading. Major exchanges often have high liquidity, which means there are enough buyers and sellers to ensure smooth and timely transactions.
- **User Experience**: User-friendly interfaces and tools are essential for a seamless trading experience. A well-designed exchange makes it easier for users to navigate and execute trades.
- **Security:** Security measures vary between exchanges. Factors to consider include the implementation of two-factor authentication (2FA), cold storage of funds, and the exchange's history of security breaches.
- **Fees:** Exchanges charge fees for various services, including trading, withdrawals, and deposits. The fee structure can significantly impact the cost of trading and should be considered when choosing an exchange.
- **Regulation:** Some exchanges adhere to regulatory standards and compliance, while others operate in a less regulated environment. Users should be aware of the regulatory status of the exchange they choose.

2.2.1   Types of Cryptocurrency Wallets

Cryptocurrency wallets are essential tools for managing and storing digital assets. They come in two primary categories:

hot wallets and cold wallets. Understanding the distinctions between these wallet types is vital for securely storing and accessing your cryptocurrencies.

Hot Wallets

Hot wallets are digital wallets that are connected to the internet and can be accessed via web browsers, mobile applications, or other online means. They are convenient for day-to-day cryptocurrency transactions, such as sending and receiving funds. However, they are more susceptible to hacking and online threats. Here are the main types of hot wallets:

- **Software Wallets**: These are online or mobile wallets that store your private keys on your device or in the cloud. They are easy to use but may be vulnerable to security breaches if your device is compromised or if you fall victim to phishing attacks.
- **Exchange Wallets:** Many cryptocurrency exchanges provide built-in wallets for users to store their assets on the platform. While these are convenient, it's important to remember that assets stored on an exchange are under the exchange's control, not yours. Exchanges have been targeted by hackers in the past, resulting in losses for users.

Cold Wallets

Cold wallets are offline storage solutions that offer a higher level of security because they are not connected to the internet. This reduces the risk of hacking and unauthorized access. Two common types of cold wallets are:

- **Hardware Wallets:** These are physical devices designed specifically for securely storing cryptocurrencies. They are considered one of the most secure options for long-term storage of significant cryptocurrency holdings. Hardware wallets store private keys offline and require physical interaction for transactions.
- **Paper Wallets:** A paper wallet is a physical piece of paper that contains your cryptocurrency's private and

public keys. It is entirely offline, making it immune to online threats. Paper wallets are a cost-effective way to store cryptocurrencies securely, but they require careful handling and safeguarding to avoid loss.

Balancing the convenience of hot wallets for everyday transactions with the security of cold storage for long-term asset protection is a key consideration in managing your cryptocurrency portfolio. In the subsequent sections of this chapter, we will delve deeper into the security considerations and best practices for cryptocurrency storage. Understanding these concepts will help you safeguard your assets effectively.

2.3 Cold Storage vs. Hot Storage

The choice between cold storage and hot storage is a critical decision when it comes to safeguarding your cryptocurrency holdings. Each method has its advantages and disadvantages, making it important to strike a balance between security and accessibility based on your specific needs.

Cold Storage:

Cold storage involves keeping your cryptocurrency offline, disconnected from the internet. This approach provides a significant reduction in the risk of hacking or unauthorized access. The main types of cold storage include hardware wallets and paper wallets:

- **Hardware Wallets**: These physical devices are designed specifically for securely storing cryptocurrencies. They store private keys offline, making them one of the most secure options for long-term storage of significant cryptocurrency holdings. Hardware wallets require physical interaction to initiate transactions, adding an extra layer of protection.
- **Paper Wallets**: A paper wallet is a physical piece of paper

that contains your cryptocurrency's private and public keys. It is entirely offline, which makes it immune to online threats. Paper wallets are a cost-effective way to store cryptocurrencies securely, but they require careful handling and safeguarding to avoid loss.

Cold storage is ideal for storing large amounts of cryptocurrency for the long term. The fact that your private keys are not connected to the internet significantly reduces the risk of them being compromised.

Hot Storage:

Hot storage refers to keeping your cryptocurrency in online wallets that are connected to the internet. While hot wallets are more convenient for everyday transactions, they are also more vulnerable to online threats, such as hacking and phishing attacks. Common types of hot wallets include online wallets and mobile wallets:

- **Online Wallets**: These are digital wallets accessible through web browsers and are often provided by cryptocurrency exchange platforms. They are suitable for quick transactions but should not be used for long-term storage of substantial amounts.
- **Mobile Wallets**: Mobile wallets are smartphone applications that enable easy access to your cryptocurrency on the go. They are practical for daily use but come with the risk of loss or theft if your device is compromised.

Balancing Cold and Hot Storage:

A common approach adopted by many cryptocurrency enthusiasts is to strike a balance between the security of cold storage and the convenience of hot storage. They keep the majority of their assets in cold storage, which is securely tucked away offline, while maintaining a smaller portion in hot wallets for active trading and spending. This way, they can access and use their cryptocurrency for daily transactions while ensuring that the majority of their holdings remain safe from online threats.

In the upcoming chapters of this eBook, we will delve deeper into various aspects of cryptocurrency, including investment strategies, security best practices, regulatory considerations, and the potential impact of cryptocurrencies on the global financial landscape. A comprehensive understanding of these topics will empower you to navigate the world of cryptocurrencies more effectively and make informed decisions.

3.0 CHAPTER 3: INVESTING AND TRADING

In this chapter, we will explore the world of cryptocurrency investment and trading. Understanding different investment strategies, trading approaches, and the associated risks and rewards is essential for anyone looking to make informed decisions in the cryptocurrency space.

3.1 Investment Strategies in Cryptocurrencies

Investing in cryptocurrencies is not just about buying and holding; it involves a range of strategies tailored to individual goals, risk tolerance, and time horizons. Here are some common investment strategies to consider:

HODLing: This strategy involves buying a cryptocurrency and holding onto it for the long term, regardless of short-term price fluctuations. HODLers believe in the long-term potential of their chosen assets.

- **Diversification**: Diversifying your cryptocurrency portfolio involves spreading your investments across multiple digital assets. This strategy helps reduce risk and exposure to the price volatility of any single cryptocurrency.
- **Day Trading**: Day traders aim to profit from short-term price fluctuations by making multiple trades within a

single day. This strategy requires a deep understanding of market trends and technical analysis.

- **Swing Trading:** Swing traders take advantage of price swings or "swings" in the market. They aim to capitalize on short to medium-term price movements, holding positions for days or weeks.

Value Investing: Similar to traditional value investing, this strategy involves identifying undervalued cryptocurrencies with strong fundamentals and long-term potential.

- **Buy and Hold (Long-Term Investing):** This is a conservative strategy that involves investing in cryptocurrencies with solid fundamentals and holding them for an extended period, often years.

3.2 Day Trading vs. HODLing

Day trading and HODLing represent two contrasting approaches to cryptocurrency investment and trading.

- **Day Trading:** Day traders buy and sell cryptocurrencies within the same day, seeking to profit from short-term price movements. This approach requires constant monitoring of the market, technical analysis skills, and the ability to react quickly. It can be highly profitable but also comes with a significant risk of loss due to the volatile nature of cryptocurrencies.

- **HODLing:** HODLers are long-term investors who believe in the potential of their chosen cryptocurrencies and are willing to hold onto them for an extended period, often through market fluctuations. HODLing can be less stressful and time-consuming than day trading, but it requires patience and the ability to weather price volatility.

Choosing between day trading and HODLing depends on your risk tolerance, time commitment, and trading experience. Many investors combine these strategies, allocating a portion of their portfolio to HODLing while actively trading with the rest.

3.3 Risks and Rewards

Cryptocurrency investment and trading offer both potential rewards and significant risks. It's essential to be aware of these factors before diving into the market:

Rewards:

Profit Potential: Cryptocurrencies have delivered substantial returns over the years, and successful investors have reaped significant profits.

Diversification: The cryptocurrency market offers a variety of assets with different use cases, potentially allowing you to diversify your portfolio.

Accessibility: The cryptocurrency market is open 24/7, providing flexibility for traders and investors.

Risks:

- **Volatility:** Cryptocurrencies are known for their price volatility, which can lead to rapid gains but also substantial losses.
- **Regulatory Uncertainty**: Cryptocurrency regulations vary by region and may change, impacting the market.
- **Security Concerns:** The risk of hacks, scams, and the loss of assets due to technical issues is ever-present.
- **Lack of Fundamentals**: Many cryptocurrencies lack a track record, making it challenging to assess their long-term potential.

Understanding these risks and rewards is essential for making informed decisions in the cryptocurrency market. In the upcoming sections of this chapter, we will explore these topics in more detail, providing you with the knowledge to develop your own cryptocurrency investment and trading strategy.

4.0 CHAPTER 4: MINING AND STAKING

In this chapter, we will delve into the fascinating world of cryptocurrency mining and staking. These two processes are fundamental to the operation of many blockchain networks, providing security, validating transactions, and earning rewards. We will also explore the environmental impact of mining and how it has become a topic of global concern.

4.1 What is Mining and How it Works

Mining is a fundamental process in the world of cryptocurrencies. It serves a dual purpose: validating transactions and maintaining the security and integrity of the blockchain. Miners play a crucial role in this ecosystem, and the process by which they achieve this is nothing short of remarkable. As miners collect and validate transactions, they act as the gatekeepers of the cryptocurrency network, ensuring that only legitimate transactions are added to the blockchain. These transactions are then bundled into blocks, which form the building blocks of the blockchain itself.

Proof of Work (PoW) is the prevailing consensus algorithm used by most cryptocurrencies. It's the engine that powers the mining process. Miners must race to solve a complex cryptographic puzzle, a process that requires immense computational power. The first miner to successfully solve this puzzle gets the privilege of adding the new block to the blockchain.

Rewards are the driving force for miners. In return for their hard work and computational resources, miners receive a reward. This reward typically includes newly minted cryptocurrency, which serves to introduce new coins into circulation, and transaction fees paid by users. It's this combination of incentives that keeps the mining process running smoothly.

Consensus is a critical aspect of the mining process. Once a miner successfully adds a block to the blockchain, the network participants must reach a consensus on the state of the ledger. This consensus ensures that all nodes in the network agree on the sequence and validity of transactions, preventing any single entity from controlling or manipulating the blockchain. This process repeats continuously, as miners collectively maintain the cryptocurrency network. Their efforts are what underpin the trust and security users have in the system. The fascinating world of mining is constantly evolving, with new mining hardware, improved algorithms, and an ever-expanding network of miners striving to keep the blockchain operational.

4.2 Staking and Earning Passive Income

Staking represents a departure from the energy-intensive Proof of Work mining model, offering an alternative way for individuals to participate in cryptocurrency networks. It introduces a concept known as Proof of Stake (PoS), where users can "stake" their cryptocurrency holdings to help secure and validate the network. This innovative approach has gained traction, especially with the transition of major cryptocurrencies like Ethereum from PoW to PoS.

To engage in staking, users commit a specific amount of cryptocurrency as collateral, effectively locking it up in a smart contract. This collateral is essential for ensuring that validators, the participants responsible for proposing and validating new blocks, have a vested interest in maintaining the network's security and integrity. The higher the stake, the greater the chance of being chosen as a validator.

Block proposal and validation in PoS networks differ from PoW. Validators are chosen to propose new blocks based on various factors, which may include the amount of cryptocurrency they've staked, their reputation in the network, or a combination of such criteria. This selection process aims to ensure that those with a genuine interest in the network's stability are the ones contributing.

Block validation, as in PoW, remains a fundamental aspect of the consensus mechanism. Validators work together to verify the validity of proposed blocks. If a proposed block is accepted, it becomes a part of the blockchain, and the validator responsible is rewarded with additional cryptocurrency.

Earning passive income through staking has become an attractive option for those looking to be a part of the cryptocurrency ecosystem without the energy and resource-intensive demands of mining. However, staking isn't without its complexities, and the details can vary among different PoS cryptocurrencies.

4.3 The Environmental Impact of Mining

Cryptocurrency mining, particularly in Proof of Work (PoW) systems, has increasingly faced scrutiny due to its significant energy consumption and the associated environmental consequences. It's essential to understand the environmental impact to make informed decisions in the world of cryptocurrencies.

The energy-intensive nature of PoW mining, particularly in the case of major cryptocurrencies like Bitcoin, is a result of the need for computational power to solve complex cryptographic puzzles. This requires substantial electricity consumption, which can be a strain on power resources, especially in regions where cryptocurrencies are mined at scale.

A notable concern is the carbon emissions associated with mining operations, particularly in areas where electricity is generated using fossil fuels such as coal. The carbon footprint of these operations has raised environmental alarms, contributing to global concerns about the sustainability of cryptocurrency networks.

Efforts are underway to address these concerns. Some cryptocurrencies are transitioning from PoW to Proof of Stake (PoS), which is considered more energy-efficient. Ethereum, one of the largest blockchain networks, is in the process of moving to PoS with its Ethereum 2.0 upgrade. This transition aims to significantly reduce the energy consumption associated with maintaining the network.

Furthermore, there are initiatives to make cryptocurrency mining more environmentally friendly. Some mining operations are increasingly seeking to use renewable energy sources, such as solar or wind power, to power their operations. This shift toward "green mining" is seen as a step in the right direction to mitigate the environmental impact of cryptocurrency activities.

As the cryptocurrency industry continues to evolve, finding a balance between the benefits of blockchain technology and sustainability remains a priority. Being aware of the environmental impact of mining is crucial in this ongoing conversation.

5.0 CHAPTER 5: INITIAL COIN OFFERINGS (ICOS) AND TOKENS

In this chapter, we will embark on a journey into the dynamic world of Initial Coin Offerings (ICOs) and tokens. ICOs represented a groundbreaking fundraising method for blockchain-based projects, and they played a significant role in the cryptocurrency space's evolution. We will explore the concept of ICOs, their meteoric rise, and subsequent challenges. Additionally, we'll delve into the distinction between utility tokens and security tokens, two prominent categories of tokens that emerged from this innovative fundraising mechanism.

5.1 What are ICOs?

Initial Coin Offerings, commonly abbreviated as ICOs, were a novel fundraising method used by blockchain projects and startups to raise capital. They enabled these projects to bypass traditional financial institutions and directly appeal to the global community of cryptocurrency enthusiasts for funding. ICOs typically revolved around the issuance and sale of a new cryptocurrency, often referred to as a token, as a means of raising funds for development.

Here's a closer look at how ICOs worked:
- **Token Creation:** The project initiating the ICO would

create a new cryptocurrency token, which would often have specific use cases within their ecosystem. These tokens could represent ownership, access, or some utility within the project's platform.

- **Fundraising:** During the ICO event, the project would offer these newly created tokens to the public, typically in exchange for established cryptocurrencies like Bitcoin or Ethereum. Participants in the ICO would send these cryptocurrencies to the project's designated wallet address and receive the new tokens in return.

- **Use of Funds**: The funds raised through the ICO would be allocated to various aspects of project development, such as technology, marketing, and legal compliance. This capital injection was essential for blockchain projects to bring their vision to life.

- **Community Engagement**: ICOs were known for their ability to engage and mobilize a global community of supporters. Projects often maintained active communication with their community, building a loyal following and fostering enthusiasm for the project's success.

5.2 The Rise and Fall of ICOs

The rise of ICOs was nothing short of a revolution in the world of fundraising. It provided an accessible and decentralized method for startups to gather substantial capital quickly. During the ICO craze of 2017 and early 2018, numerous projects raised billions of dollars in a matter of months.

However, with great promise came substantial challenges and concerns:

- **Lack of Regulation**: The absence of clear regulatory frameworks in the early days of ICOs led to a proliferation of scams and fraudulent projects. Investors were exposed to significant risks due to the lack of oversight.

- **Speculative Mania**: The meteoric rise in the value of cryptocurrencies and the potential for quick, substantial gains led to a speculative frenzy. Many participants entered the space solely to make a profit, often without a deep understanding of the projects they were investing in.
- **Legal Scrutiny:** As the regulatory landscape began to take shape, many ICOs faced legal scrutiny and enforcement actions. Authorities worldwide aimed to protect investors and maintain financial stability.
- **Erosion of Trust:** Due to the proliferation of scams and fraudulent projects, trust in the ICO space eroded. Investors became more cautious, and the enthusiasm that characterized the early ICO days waned.

In response to these challenges, the ICO landscape underwent a transformation. Many projects shifted their fundraising models, and regulatory compliance became a priority. The era of the ICO evolved into a new phase, giving rise to alternative fundraising methods such as Security Token Offerings (STOs) and Initial Exchange Offerings (IEOs).

5.3 Utility Tokens vs. Security Tokens

One of the defining aspects of ICOs was the creation of different types of tokens. The two primary categories that emerged from ICOs are utility tokens and security tokens.

- **Utility Tokens:** Utility tokens are designed to provide access to a project's platform, services, or products. They often have specific use cases within the project's ecosystem. For example, utility tokens might be used to pay for transaction fees, access features, or participate in the governance of a blockchain network.
- **Security Tokens:** Security tokens, on the other hand, represent ownership in an underlying asset, such as

equity in a company, debt, or real estate. They are deemed as investment contracts and are subject to securities regulations. Security tokens often entitle their holders to dividends, revenue share, or other financial benefits derived from the project's success.

The distinction between utility tokens and security tokens is crucial, as it determines the regulatory requirements and the rights and protections provided to token holders. The classification of a token can have significant legal and financial implications. As the cryptocurrency space continues to evolve, understanding the nature and purpose of different types of tokens is essential for both investors and project developers.

In the following sections of this chapter, we will explore the impact of ICOs on the blockchain industry and the evolving landscape of token offerings. We will also delve into the legal and regulatory considerations surrounding security tokens and how these developments are shaping the future of fundraising in the cryptocurrency space.

6.0 CHAPTER 6: SECURITY AND RISKS

In this chapter, we will delve into the critical aspects of security within the cryptocurrency space. The world of digital assets, while full of opportunities, also presents significant security risks. Understanding common threats, learning how to safeguard your investments, and implementing essential security measures is paramount in ensuring the safety of your cryptocurrency holdings.

6.1 COMMON SECURITY THREATS

Cryptocurrency investments are vulnerable to a range of security threats. Being aware of these threats is the first step toward protecting your assets. Here are some of the most prevalent security risks:

- Hacks: Cryptocurrency exchanges, wallets, and even entire blockchains can be vulnerable to hacking. Malicious actors often target platforms with weak security measures, resulting in the theft of user funds.
- **Scams:** The cryptocurrency space has seen its fair share of scams, including Ponzi schemes, fake ICOs, and fraudulent investment opportunities. These scams can deceive investors and lead to significant financial losses.
- **Phishing:** Phishing attacks involve tricking individuals into revealing their private keys or sensitive information by impersonating legitimate websites, wallets, or services. Phishing emails and websites can be highly convincing, making it essential to exercise caution.
- **Social Engineering:** Some attacks involve manipulating individuals into revealing sensitive information or transferring funds. These attacks can target the individual directly, attempting to exploit trust or fear to achieve their goals.
- **Malware and Keyloggers:** Malicious software can infect your device, monitor your keystrokes, and gain access to your cryptocurrency holdings. This type of attack is often delivered through email attachments or

compromised websites.

6.2 How to Protect Your Investments

Protecting your cryptocurrency investments is a top priority. Here are some fundamental steps to enhance security:

- **Use Reputable Services**: Choose well-established and reputable cryptocurrency exchanges and wallet providers. Research their security measures and user feedback to make informed choices.
- **Cold Storage**: Consider using hardware wallets for long-term storage of significant cryptocurrency holdings. Hardware wallets are offline devices that provide a high level of security by keeping your private keys away from the internet.
- **Two-Factor Authentication (2FA)**: Enable 2FA on your cryptocurrency exchange and wallet accounts. This extra layer of security helps prevent unauthorized access to your accounts, even if your login credentials are compromised.
- **Secure Passwords**: Use strong, unique passwords for each of your cryptocurrency accounts. Consider using a reputable password manager to generate and store complex passwords securely.
- **Regular Updates**: Keep your software, operating systems, and antivirus programs up to date to defend against potential vulnerabilities that could be exploited by hackers.
- **Beware of Phishing:** Exercise caution when clicking on links and opening attachments in emails. Ensure you are on legitimate websites by verifying the web address, and do not share sensitive information with unverified sources.

6.3　TWO-FACTOR AUTHENTICATION AND HARDWARE WALLETS

- Two-Factor Authentication (2FA): 2FA adds an additional layer of security to your accounts by requiring a second form of verification beyond your password. This often involves receiving a one-time code on your mobile device, which must be entered to access your account. Most cryptocurrency exchanges and wallets offer 2FA as an option.

- Hardware Wallets: Hardware wallets are considered one of the most secure methods for storing cryptocurrencies. These physical devices store your private keys offline, making them inaccessible to hackers. Popular hardware wallet brands include Ledger and Trezor. If you have significant cryptocurrency holdings, investing in a hardware wallet is a wise choice for long-term storage.

Understanding the security threats in the cryptocurrency space and implementing the necessary protective measures is vital for the safety of your investments. In the following chapters, we will explore the dynamic world of decentralized finance (DeFi), delve deeper into the technical aspects of blockchain technology, and investigate the evolving landscape of the cryptocurrency market.

7.0 CHAPTER 7: REGULATION AND LEGAL FRAMEWORK

In this chapter, we will explore the evolving landscape of cryptocurrency regulation and the legal frameworks that govern digital assets around the world. The relationship between cryptocurrency and the law is complex and multifaceted. We will delve into how different countries approach regulation, the role of anti-money laundering (AML) and Know Your Customer (KYC) laws, and the significance of government and regulatory bodies in shaping the legal framework for cryptocurrencies.

7.1 Cryptocurrency Regulation by Country

Cryptocurrency regulation varies significantly from one country to another. Some countries have embraced digital currencies and have developed clear regulatory frameworks, while others have adopted a more cautious or restrictive approach. Here's a glimpse into the global regulatory landscape:

- **Cryptocurrency-Friendly Countries**: Some nations have positioned themselves as cryptocurrency-friendly hubs, offering a conducive environment for blockchain and crypto businesses. Examples include Switzerland, Singapore, Malta, and Estonia, which have developed comprehensive regulatory frameworks that provide legal certainty and encourage innovation.
- **Strict Regulatory Countries**: On the other end of the

spectrum, certain countries have imposed stringent regulations and even outright bans on cryptocurrencies. China, for instance, has banned initial coin offerings (ICOs) and cryptocurrency exchanges, and India has experienced regulatory uncertainty, which has led to significant restrictions on crypto activities.

- **The United States:** The U.S. is known for its complex and evolving regulatory environment. Various federal agencies, such as the Securities and Exchange Commission (SEC) and the Commodity Futures Trading Commission (CFTC), oversee different aspects of cryptocurrencies. Additionally, individual states have introduced their own regulations, creating a patchwork of rules and requirements.

- **European Union (EU):** The EU has taken steps to provide a unified regulatory framework for cryptocurrencies across its member states. The Fifth Anti-Money Laundering Directive (5AMLD) has extended AML and KYC regulations to crypto businesses, bringing them under the same compliance standards as traditional financial institutions.

7.2 Anti-Money Laundering (AML) and Know Your Customer (KYC) Laws

Anti-money laundering (AML) and Know Your Customer (KYC) laws play a crucial role in cryptocurrency regulation. These laws are designed to combat illegal activities, such as money laundering and terrorist financing, and to enhance transparency in the cryptocurrency space. Key points to consider:

- **AML Regulations:** Cryptocurrency businesses, including exchanges and wallet providers, are often required to implement AML measures. This includes verifying the identity of users, monitoring transactions for suspicious activity, and reporting such activity to authorities.

- **KYC Requirements:** Know Your Customer (KYC) procedures involve verifying the identity of users through the collection of personal information, such as government-issued identification and proof of address. These requirements help ensure that cryptocurrency transactions are conducted by legitimate individuals and entities.

7.3 THE ROLE OF GOVERNMENT AND REGULATORY BODIES

Government agencies and regulatory bodies play a pivotal role in shaping the legal framework for cryptocurrencies. Their responsibilities include:

- **Creating Regulations**: Governments and regulatory bodies are responsible for formulating and implementing regulations related to cryptocurrencies. These regulations can vary widely, covering issues like taxation, securities laws, and consumer protection.

- **Enforcing Laws**: Regulatory bodies enforce cryptocurrency laws and regulations, taking action against entities or individuals that fail to comply with legal requirements. Enforcement can include fines, penalties, and even criminal charges.

- **Educating the Public:** Governments and regulatory bodies also have a role in educating the public about the risks and benefits of cryptocurrencies. This may include issuing warnings about potential scams or frauds.

- **International Cooperation**: Given the global nature of cryptocurrencies, international cooperation is essential. Regulatory bodies often collaborate with their counterparts in other countries to address cross-border issues and develop consistent regulatory standards.

As the cryptocurrency space continues to evolve, regulation and legal frameworks will remain a dynamic and critical aspect of the industry. Understanding the regulatory landscape in your country and staying informed about international developments is essential for both cryptocurrency enthusiasts and businesses. In the subsequent chapters, we will explore the innovative world of decentralized finance (DeFi), discuss the technical aspects of blockchain technology, and analyze the potential impact of cryptocurrencies on the global financial landscape.

8.0 CHAPTER 8: ALTCOINS AND TOKENS

In this chapter, we will explore the vast and diverse world of altcoins and tokens. Altcoins, which stands for "alternative coins," encompass all cryptocurrencies other than Bitcoin. Additionally, we will delve into the various types of tokens that exist within the cryptocurrency space. We'll provide an overview of some prominent projects and their use cases, and discuss the importance of diversifying your cryptocurrency portfolio.

8.1 An Overview of Altcoins and Tokens

Altcoins, a term derived from "alternative coins," represent a diverse category of cryptocurrencies that goes beyond the trailblazing Bitcoin. While Bitcoin was the original and most widely recognized digital currency, its success paved the way for the creation of numerous alternative cryptocurrencies, each with its distinctive features, use cases, and underlying technologies. Among the multitude of altcoins, several common types have emerged, each addressing different aspects of the cryptocurrency and blockchain landscape:

- **Ethereum and Smart Contract Platforms**: Ethereum, launched in 2015 by Vitalik Buterin, introduced a groundbreaking concept to the world of cryptocurrencies: smart contracts. Smart contracts are self-executing agreements with the terms of the contract directly written into code. These contracts enable the development of decentralized applications (DApps) that can perform a wide range of functions without the need for intermediaries. Ethereum's innovation spurred the growth of decentralized finance (DeFi), a new financial ecosystem built on blockchain technology. Ethereum's native cryptocurrency, Ether (ETH), serves as both a digital currency and a fuel for executing smart contracts. The Ethereum blockchain has become a hub for various DApps, DeFi protocols, and non-fungible tokens (NFTs).

- **Privacy Coins**: Privacy coins are designed to enhance user anonymity and transaction privacy. These coins utilize advanced cryptographic techniques to obfuscate transaction details, making it extremely difficult to trace the sender, recipient, or transaction amount. Examples of privacy-focused coins include Monero (XMR) and Zcash (ZEC). Monero, for instance, employs ring signatures and confidential transactions to provide enhanced privacy. Privacy coins cater to individuals who value financial privacy, whether for personal or business reasons. They are often used for transactions where confidentiality is paramount.

- **Stablecoins:** The cryptocurrency market is known for its price volatility, which can be both a boon and a bane for investors and users. Stablecoins aim to mitigate this volatility by pegging their value to traditional fiat currencies like the US dollar or assets like gold. Tether (USDT), USD Coin (USDC), BUSD and DAI are examples of stablecoins. Stablecoins provide a stable store of value within the cryptocurrency ecosystem and serve as a bridge between the crypto and traditional financial worlds. They are commonly used for trading, remittances, and as a safe haven during periods of high market volatility.

- **Utility Tokens:** Utility tokens, sometimes referred to as app coins or user tokens, are designed to provide access to specific services, features, or functions within a blockchain-based platform or ecosystem. Holders of these tokens can use them to pay for transaction fees, access DApps, or participate in platform governance. One well-known utility token is Binance Coin (BNB), which can be used to pay trading fees on the Binance exchange, participate in token sales on the Binance Launchpad, and more. Another example is Chainlink (LINK), which is used to incentivize and reward participants in the Chainlink network, ensuring the reliability of off-chain data for smart contracts.

- **Security Tokens**: Security tokens represent ownership in real-world assets, such as real estate, company equity, or commodities. Unlike utility tokens, they are categorized as securities and are subject to regulatory compliance. Security tokens often provide their holders with ownership rights, dividends, or profit-sharing, similar to traditional financial instruments. The issuance and trading of security tokens are governed by securities laws and regulations. Compliance with Know Your Customer (KYC) and Anti-Money Laundering (AML) requirements is essential. Security tokens have the potential to bridge the gap between traditional finance and the blockchain world by offering fractional ownership and increased liquidity for assets that were previously illiquid.

Understanding the various types of altcoins and tokens is crucial for investors and enthusiasts. Each type serves a different purpose within the broader cryptocurrency and blockchain ecosystem, and their features and use cases can significantly impact their value and adoption. Additionally, the regulatory implications of different token categories must be considered when engaging with them.

8.2 Prominent Projects and Their Use Cases

The world of cryptocurrencies extends well beyond Bitcoin and includes numerous projects that have gained recognition for their innovative use cases and the strong communities supporting them. These prominent altcoins and tokens have carved their niches within the cryptocurrency space, each with a unique value proposition. In this section, we'll delve into a selection of these projects and explore their respective use cases.

- **Ripple (XRP):** Ripple, often associated with its digital asset XRP, is a blockchain-based payment protocol with a primary focus on facilitating cross-border payments for financial institutions. One of the main problems Ripple aims to address is the inefficiency and cost associated with traditional international money transfers. Swift, the conventional system used by banks for cross-border transactions, can be slow and expensive. Ripple offers a faster, more cost-effective alternative.

XRP, the native cryptocurrency of the Ripple network, plays a crucial role as a bridge currency for facilitating cross-border payments. By using XRP as an intermediary, financial institutions can conduct cross-border transactions with reduced fees and shorter settlement times. Ripple's solutions have gained adoption by various banks and payment service providers worldwide, marking a significant shift in the way traditional finance handles cross-border remittances.

- **Litecoin (LTC):** Often referred to as *digital silver* in the cryptocurrency community, Litecoin is a peer-to-peer digital currency created by Charlie Lee. Litecoin shares many similarities with Bitcoin, such as its use as a digital store of value and medium of exchange. However, it distinguishes itself through faster transaction confirmation times and a different hashing algorithm. Litecoin uses the Scrypt proof-of-work algorithm, which is considered less resource-intensive than Bitcoin's SHA-256 algorithm. This design results in quicker block generation times and lower transaction confirmation times. Litecoin's faster settlement times make it suitable for everyday transactions and microtransactions. While Bitcoin remains a prominent store of value, Litecoin has carved out its niche by focusing on efficient and rapid transactions, positioning itself as a viable option for those looking for a digital currency for everyday use.

- **Cardano (ADA):** Cardano is a blockchain platform that emphasizes security, sustainability, and interoperability. Founded by Charles Hoskinson, one of the co-founders of Ethereum, Cardano's development is driven by a strong academic and research-oriented approach. The project's goal is to provide a secure and scalable infrastructure for the development of decentralized applications (DApps) and smart contracts.

Cardano's unique approach involves separating the settlement and computation layers of its blockchain, enhancing security and scalability. The platform has a focus on formal verification, which aims to mathematically prove the correctness of smart contracts, reducing the risk of vulnerabilities and security breaches. Furthermore, Cardano utilizes a proof-of-stake (PoS) consensus mechanism, which is energy-efficient compared to Bitcoin's proof-of-work. Cardano's commitment to sustainability and security positions it as a blockchain platform for building secure and scalable DApps. It has attracted a growing developer community and a dedicated following.

- **Polkadot (DOT):** Polkadot is a multi-chain network designed to enable interoperability among different blockchains. It was created by Dr. Gavin Wood, one of the co-founders of Ethereum, and aims to solve the issue of blockchain fragmentation by connecting various blockchains into a unified network. Polkadot is a protocol that allows different blockchains to communicate, share data, and transact with one another. The unique aspect of Polkadot is its parachain architecture, which allows individual blockchains (parachains) to connect to the Polkadot relay chain. This approach enables greater scalability and flexibility, as it reduces congestion on individual blockchains and allows them to benefit from the security and consensus mechanisms of the Polkadot network. Polkadot's vision is to create a decentralized, scalable, and interconnected web, where different blockchains can specialize in specific functions while maintaining seamless communication and data transfer.

- **Uniswap (UNI):** Uniswap is a decentralized exchange (DEX) built on the Ethereum blockchain. DEXs differ from centralized exchanges as they do not rely on intermediaries to facilitate transactions. Uniswap is particularly known for its automated market maker (AMM) model, which allows users to swap various cryptocurrencies directly from their wallets without the need for an order book or a traditional intermediary.

The UNI token plays a central role in the Uniswap ecosystem. Token holders have governance rights and can participate in the decision-making process for the protocol. Users can provide liquidity to the exchange by depositing cryptocurrency pairs into liquidity pools and earn fees in return. Uniswap has gained significant popularity within the decentralized finance (DeFi) space, offering users access to a wide range of cryptocurrency assets and enabling permissionless trading and liquidity provision. Its success has contributed to the growth of the DeFi ecosystem and highlighted the potential of DEXs.

Understanding these prominent projects and their respective use cases provides insights into the diverse applications of blockchain technology and cryptocurrencies. Each project has addressed unique challenges and opportunities within the crypto space, catering to different user needs and preferences. This diversity contributes to the overall growth and maturation of the cryptocurrency ecosystem, offering a range of choices for investors and enthusiasts.

8.3 Diversifying Your Portfolio

In the ever-evolving landscape of the cryptocurrency market, diversification stands out as a fundamental strategy for managing risk and enhancing the potential for gains. Diversifying your portfolio involves spreading your investments across a variety of cryptocurrencies and tokens, mitigating the exposure to price fluctuations associated with any single asset. By embracing diversification, you aim to harness the unique strengths and growth prospects of different projects and asset types.

8.3.1 The Rationale for Diversification

Diversification has long been regarded as a wise investment

strategy across various asset classes, and it holds particular significance in the context of cryptocurrencies. Here's why it's crucial:

- **Risk Mitigation:** The cryptocurrency market is known for its inherent volatility. Prices can exhibit extreme fluctuations in short periods, which can lead to significant gains or losses. By diversifying, you can reduce the impact of adverse price movements in any single asset, thus protecting your overall portfolio value.
- **Exposure to Innovation**: The blockchain and cryptocurrency space is continually evolving. Innovative projects with unique features and purposes emerge regularly. By diversifying, you can gain exposure to the potential growth and innovation brought forth by different projects, not limiting yourself to the success or failure of a single cryptocurrency.
- **Purpose-Specific Investments**: Various cryptocurrencies serve different functions. Some aim to be digital cash, while others focus on smart contracts, privacy, or stable value. Diversification enables you to allocate investments according to different use cases, offering a balanced approach to various aspects of the blockchain ecosystem.
- **Reduced Single-Asset Dependence**: Depending heavily on a single cryptocurrency may leave your portfolio susceptible to its specific vulnerabilities or market dynamics. Diversification spreads these risks across multiple assets, making your investments more resilient.

8.3.2 How to Diversify Your Portfolio

Diversification should be approached thoughtfully and backed by research. It's not merely about allocating funds randomly but understanding the projects you invest in. Here's how to diversify your cryptocurrency portfolio:

- **Project Fundamentals:** Research and evaluate the

fundamentals of the projects you're interested in. Assess their technology, use case, team, and community support. Strong fundamentals can indicate the potential for long-term viability and growth.

- **Asset Types:** Consider different categories of cryptocurrencies and tokens, including established cryptocurrencies like Bitcoin and Ethereum, newer promising projects, stablecoins, utility tokens, and more. Each category brings unique benefits and risks.
- **Risk Tolerance:** Tailor your diversification strategy to your risk tolerance. If you're more risk-averse, you might allocate a larger portion of your portfolio to established and stable assets. If you're willing to embrace higher risk for potentially higher rewards, you may consider allocating more to emerging projects.
- **Portfolio Allocation:** Diversification doesn't mean spreading your investments evenly across all assets. Allocate your funds based on your risk tolerance and confidence in the projects. Some investors choose to hold a core position in well-established cryptocurrencies and allocate smaller portions to riskier, high-potential assets.
- **Rebalancing:** Regularly reassess your portfolio and adjust your allocations as needed. Over time, the cryptocurrency market may experience shifts in the performance of different assets. Rebalancing helps you maintain your desired risk-reward profile.
- **Stay Informed:** The cryptocurrency market is dynamic, and staying informed is essential for effective diversification. Keep track of the latest developments, emerging trends, and potential opportunities in the crypto space.

8.3.3   The Role of Diversification in Risk Management

Diversifying your cryptocurrency portfolio does not eliminate risk, but it spreads it across different assets.

This risk distribution can mitigate the potential impact of losses from a poorly performing asset. The rationale behind diversification in risk management is to ensure that the gains from well-performing assets outweigh the losses from underperforming ones. It's essential to maintain a balanced and well-diversified portfolio. Avoid concentrating too much in a single asset class or project, as it can expose your investments to undue risk. Keep in mind that diversification should align with your investment goals, risk tolerance, and time horizon.

As the cryptocurrency market continues to evolve, diversification remains a valuable strategy for navigating its inherent uncertainties. By understanding the diverse applications and value propositions of various projects, you can make informed decisions and create a portfolio tailored to your investment objectives. In the upcoming chapters, we will explore the technical aspects of blockchain technology, delve into the innovative realm of decentralized finance (DeFi), and analyze the potential implications of cryptocurrencies on the global financial landscape. Stay tuned for a deeper understanding of the cryptocurrency space.

9.0 CHAPTER 9: DECENTRALIZED FINANCE (DEFI)

In this chapter, we embark on a journey into the fascinating world of Decentralized Finance (DeFi). DeFi represents a groundbreaking development within the cryptocurrency and blockchain space, revolutionizing traditional financial systems and opening up a world of opportunities and innovations. We'll delve into the basics of DeFi, explore key DeFi applications such as yield farming, lending, and borrowing, and discuss the inherent risks and opportunities that come with this transformative movement.

9.1 What is DeFi?

Decentralized Finance (DeFi) is a rapidly evolving movement within the blockchain and cryptocurrency space that is reshaping traditional financial systems. It represents a novel approach to finance, characterized by its core principles of decentralization, transparency, and accessibility. In this chapter, we will explore the fundamental concepts of DeFi, understand its core components, and appreciate its potential to transform the financial landscape.

- **Decentralization:** At the heart of DeFi is the concept of decentralization. Unlike traditional financial systems that rely on centralized intermediaries like banks, insurance companies, and brokerage firms, DeFi leverages blockchain technology to create open and permissionless financial services. These blockchain networks, such as Ethereum, run on a decentralized infrastructure where transactions and data are verified and recorded across a network of nodes rather than by a single centralized entity. This decentralization is key to the fundamental tenets of DeFi. It ensures that financial services are resistant to censorship, offer open access to users globally, and operate without the need for traditional financial institutions. As a result, anyone with an internet connection can participate in the DeFi ecosystem, granting financial access to those who were previously excluded from the traditional financial world.

- **Smart Contracts:** One of the defining features of DeFi is the extensive use of smart contracts. Smart contracts are self-executing agreements with predefined rules that are encoded into computer programs. These contracts facilitate, verify, or enforce the negotiation or performance of a contract, eliminating the need for intermediaries. In the context of DeFi, they play a central role in automating and securing financial transactions.

For example, in a DeFi lending platform, a smart contract can be created to automate the process of lending and borrowing. When a user deposits cryptocurrency into the platform, the smart contract ensures that the lending terms, including interest rates and collateral requirements, are met without the need for a centralized entity to oversee the transaction. This trustless nature of smart contracts fosters transparency and removes the requirement for users to rely on a third party.

- **Interoperability:** DeFi is not confined to a single platform or blockchain. Instead, it is a network of various financial applications that often interoperate with each other. This interoperability allows users to access a wide range of financial services across different DeFi platforms seamlessly. For instance, a user might lend stablecoins on one DeFi lending platform and then use those borrowed funds as liquidity in a decentralized exchange (DEX) to earn trading fees. The ability to move assets and financial opportunities between different DeFi applications adds to the flexibility and power of the DeFi ecosystem.

- **Transparency:** DeFi projects and transactions operate on open and transparent blockchain networks. Users can access and verify the data on these public ledgers, providing unparalleled transparency. This transparency builds trust among users, as they can independently audit the smart contracts, view transaction histories, and assess the security of the DeFi protocols they engage with. However, while transparency is a significant strength of DeFi, it also implies that all data, including transaction details, is publicly available. Users should be mindful of the public nature of these blockchain networks and take appropriate precautions to protect their privacy when interacting with DeFi applications.

In summary, DeFi represents a groundbreaking movement in the world of finance. It is characterized by its emphasis on decentralization, the utilization of smart contracts, interoperability, and transparency. DeFi enables open and permissionless access to financial services, fostering inclusivity and challenging the traditional financial paradigm. As we delve further into this chapter, we will explore specific DeFi applications and their functions, revealing the innovation and opportunities they bring to the world of finance.

9.2 Key DeFi Applications

Decentralized Finance (DeFi) has spawned a variety of innovative applications that offer alternatives to traditional financial services. These DeFi applications leverage blockchain technology, smart contracts, and decentralized networks to introduce new and improved ways of managing, lending, borrowing, and trading assets. In this section, we will explore some of the key DeFi applications and their functionalities.

- **Lending and Borrowing:** DeFi lending platforms have reimagined the traditional banking model. In DeFi, users can both lend their cryptocurrencies and borrow assets, all without the involvement of traditional financial institutions. Lending platforms like Compound and Aave allow users to lock up their digital assets as collateral, earning interest on the assets they supply. Meanwhile, borrowers can collateralize their holdings to secure loans. Interest rates on these platforms fluctuate based on supply and demand dynamics. The ability to lend and borrow cryptocurrency assets in a decentralized manner opens up opportunities for users to earn passive income or access liquidity without going through banks or credit institutions.

- **Decentralized Exchanges (DEXs):** Decentralized exchanges have become a cornerstone of the DeFi ecosystem, providing a secure and transparent way for users to trade cryptocurrencies. DEXs like Uniswap, SushiSwap, and PancakeSwap enable users to swap one cryptocurrency for another directly without the need for intermediaries. These platforms use automated market-making algorithms and liquidity pools to facilitate trading. By removing intermediaries, DEXs increase efficiency and reduce trading costs. They also empower users to remain in control of their assets throughout the trading process.

- **Yield Farming:** Yield farming has gained popularity as an innovative way for DeFi users to maximize their returns. This practice involves providing liquidity to DeFi platforms and earning rewards, often in the form of governance tokens or additional cryptocurrencies. Users stake their assets in liquidity pools or lending platforms, enabling these platforms to access assets for various DeFi activities. In return, users earn interest or rewards based on the amount of assets they have provided and the duration of their participation. Yield farming opens up the opportunity for users to earn passive income on their cryptocurrency holdings.

- **Stablecoins:** Stablecoins play a pivotal role in the DeFi ecosystem by providing price stability in a highly volatile crypto market. These cryptocurrencies are pegged to the value of traditional fiat currencies, such as the US Dollar (USD). Popular examples include DAI, USDC, and USDT. Stablecoins serve as a means of value preservation, enabling users to escape the price volatility of other cryptocurrencies. They are widely used for trading, remittances, and as a store of value within the DeFi space. The stability and liquidity of stablecoins make them essential for facilitating DeFi transactions and lending operations.

The rise of DeFi applications has introduced new opportunities for financial activities, offering users access to a broad spectrum of services without traditional financial intermediaries. While these DeFi applications have revolutionized the financial landscape, it's important to recognize that they come with their own set of risks and challenges. In the following section, we will delve into some of these risks and opportunities associated with DeFi.

9.3 Risks and Opportunities in DeFi

Decentralized Finance (DeFi) presents a world of opportunities for users, offering potentially high yields on assets, open access to financial services, and participation in a decentralized, borderless financial system. However, with these opportunities come inherent risks and challenges that users must carefully consider. Let's explore the risks and opportunities associated with DeFi:

- **Smart Contract Risks:** DeFi platforms rely on smart contracts, which are self-executing agreements with predefined rules. While smart contracts provide automation and transparency, they can be vulnerable to bugs and vulnerabilities. Exploits or hacks of these contracts can lead to significant financial losses. DeFi platforms must undergo rigorous code audits and testing to mitigate these risks. However, even well-audited contracts are not immune to unforeseen vulnerabilities.
- **Market Risks:** DeFi assets are often subject to extreme price volatility, which can result in substantial gains or losses for users. While the potential for high yields is an attractive aspect of DeFi, it's crucial to consider the market risks. Price swings in the cryptocurrency market can be influenced by various factors, including market sentiment, news events, and macroeconomic trends. Users should carefully assess their risk tolerance and investment strategies before participating in DeFi.

- **Regulatory Uncertainty:** The DeFi space operates within a relatively new and rapidly evolving regulatory landscape. While DeFi projects aim to provide open and borderless financial services, regulatory changes and compliance requirements can impact their operation. Governments and regulatory bodies around the world are scrutinizing DeFi, and the future regulatory environment is uncertain. Users must stay informed about the regulatory developments in their respective jurisdictions and be prepared to adapt to changing regulations.

- **Liquidity Risks:** Yield farming and liquidity provision, which involve staking assets in DeFi protocols, come with their unique set of risks. Impermanent loss is a concept in DeFi that occurs when the value of assets in a liquidity pool diverges from the value of the same assets held individually. Users should understand the dynamics of liquidity pools and the potential impact on their returns. Impermanent loss can occur when the price ratio of the assets in the pool changes significantly.

- **Counterparty Risks:** One of the core principles of DeFi is to reduce or eliminate the need for intermediaries. However, users are not entirely free from counterparty risks. They are still exposed to the risks associated with smart contract vulnerabilities, protocol failures, or governance decisions that could impact their assets. It's crucial for users to assess the security and reliability of the DeFi platforms they choose to use. Additionally, understanding the governance structure and decision-making processes of DeFi projects can help users make informed decisions.

In conclusion, DeFi has ushered in a new era of financial services and applications that challenge the traditional financial system. It offers accessibility, transparency, and programmability that have the potential to reshape the financial industry. However, users must navigate the DeFi space with caution, recognizing the risks inherent in this nascent ecosystem. As we move forward in the subsequent chapters, we will delve into the technical intricacies of blockchain technology, explore specific DeFi applications in greater detail, and assess the broader impact of cryptocurrencies on the global financial landscape. Stay tuned for a more comprehensive understanding of the crypto and blockchain world.

10.0   CHAPTER 10: THE FUTURE OF CRYPTOCURRENCY

In this final chapter, we will embark on a journey into the future of cryptocurrencies, exploring emerging technologies, scaling solutions, and making predictions for what lies ahead. The world of cryptocurrencies is ever-evolving, and understanding the developments on the horizon is crucial for anyone interested in this exciting space.

10.1   Emerging Technologies in the World of Cryptocurrencies

In the ever-evolving landscape of cryptocurrencies, innovation is the driving force that propels the industry forward. As we look to the future, several emerging technologies stand out for their potential to revolutionize the way we perceive and interact with digital assets. These technologies have already made significant waves and are poised to continue reshaping the cryptocurrency space in the years to come.

10.1.1   Non-Fungible Tokens (NFTs): Unlocking the World of Digital Ownership

Non-Fungible Tokens, commonly referred to as NFTs, have taken the digital world by storm, redefining the concept of ownership in the digital realm. NFTs represent unique digital assets, providing indisputable proof of ownership and authenticity of a specific item, piece of content, or collectible. What sets NFTs apart from traditional cryptocurrencies like Bitcoin is their indivisibility and uniqueness, making each token distinct from any other.

The application of NFTs extends across a wide array of industries, from art and gaming to entertainment and real estate. Digital artists and creators have found a groundbreaking platform to showcase their work and connect directly with their audience. NFTs have also permeated the music industry, enabling musicians to tokenize their music and merchandise, creating novel revenue streams. Furthermore, NFTs have penetrated the world of virtual real estate, giving rise to the concept of digital land ownership within virtual metaverses. Intellectual property rights are being revolutionized, with content creators and owners exploring new ways to monetize their creations through blockchain technology.

One of the most impactful aspects of NFTs is their potential to establish unalterable provenance records. This means that artists and creators can track the entire history of their work, providing an unprecedented level of transparency and trust for buyers and collectors. NFTs have the capacity to disrupt copyright and intellectual property laws by offering a technological solution for content ownership.

10.1.2 Smart Contracts: The Enablers of Trustless Transactions

Smart contracts are another groundbreaking technology within the cryptocurrency space, with their potential yet to be fully harnessed. Smart contracts are self-executing agreements with predefined rules and conditions. These contracts operate on a blockchain and automatically execute and enforce the terms of an agreement when predetermined conditions are met.

Smart contracts were initially popularized by Ethereum, which introduced the concept of decentralized applications (DApps) and the world of decentralized finance (DeFi). These agreements have the power to automate a myriad of processes, significantly reducing the need for intermediaries and enhancing trust in transactions. The rise of DeFi, a financial ecosystem built on decentralized technologies, has showcased the remarkable power of smart contracts. Within DeFi, users can lend, borrow, trade, and earn interest on their digital assets without the involvement of traditional financial institutions. Smart contracts handle the complex calculations and execute the terms of these financial transactions.

The potential applications of smart contracts extend beyond DeFi. They can be employed in various industries such as supply chain management, real estate, legal processes, and voting systems. By replacing cumbersome and often inefficient manual processes with self-executing agreements, smart contracts have the capacity to revolutionize business operations and enhance transparency and trust.

10.1.3 Decentralized Autonomous Organizations (DAOs): Shaping Decentralized Governance

Decentralized Autonomous Organizations, or DAOs, are organizations governed by code and controlled by token holders. DAOs represent a fundamental shift in the way we think about governance and decision-making. They are structured in a way that enables decentralized, community-driven management of assets and projects. The power of DAOs lies in their ability to facilitate transparent and trustless decision-making processes. Token holders in a DAO are granted voting rights based on the number of tokens they hold. Decisions related to the direction and operation of the organization are made collectively through token-holder voting, making it a truly democratic and decentralized form of governance.

DAOs have the potential to revolutionize the way businesses and projects are managed. They allow for direct community involvement and ownership, reducing the influence of centralized entities. This decentralization of power empowers users and stakeholders to have a say in the direction of a project, providing a novel approach to governance that is resistant to censorship and external control.

10.1.4   Interoperability: Bridging the Gap Between Blockchains

As the number of blockchain networks continues to proliferate, interoperability has become an increasingly vital aspect of the cryptocurrency space. Interoperability solutions aim to connect different blockchains, allowing for the seamless transfer of assets and data between these disparate ecosystems. Prominent projects like Polkadot and Cosmos are at the forefront of these efforts. Polkadot, for instance, has introduced the concept of a "multi-chain" network, which connects various blockchains to enable data and asset transfers between them. This approach enhances scalability and interoperability while preserving the individual governance of each connected chain.

Interoperability will be crucial in addressing the challenges posed by a fragmented blockchain landscape. It ensures that assets and data can flow seamlessly between different blockchains, reducing friction and promoting synergy between these networks. As the cryptocurrency industry matures, the need for interoperability will only become more pronounced.

10.2   Scaling Solutions: Enhancing the Future of

Cryptocurrencies

Scalability is a persistent challenge in the realm of cryptocurrencies. As blockchain networks continue to grow in terms of users and adoption, concerns surrounding transaction speed, cost, and energy consumption have come to the forefront. These challenges have spurred the development of various scaling solutions designed to enhance the performance of blockchain networks and meet the demands of a global user base.

10.2.1 Layer 2 Solutions: Elevating Scalability to New Heights

Layer 2 solutions represent a promising approach to addressing the scalability concerns of blockchain networks. These solutions are constructed on top of existing blockchains, with the goal of significantly increasing scalability while mitigating congestion issues. By creating an additional layer for processing transactions, Layer 2 solutions aim to alleviate the strain on the underlying blockchain, making transactions faster, more efficient, and cost-effective. One of the most notable examples of Layer 2 solutions is the Lightning Network for Bitcoin. The Lightning Network employs a network of bidirectional payment channels to facilitate rapid and low-cost transactions. By enabling users to transact off-chain and settle on the Bitcoin blockchain only when necessary, the Lightning Network significantly enhances Bitcoin's scalability.

Ethereum, another major blockchain platform, is exploring its own Layer 2 solutions, particularly Optimistic Rollups. Optimistic Rollups offer a way to scale Ethereum by processing transactions on a separate chain while ensuring the security of the main Ethereum network. This approach improves the speed and efficiency of Ethereum transactions, making it more feasible for everyday use.

10.2.2 Sharding: Breaking Down Barriers to Scalability

Sharding is another innovative solution designed to overcome the challenges of scalability by breaking down large blockchain networks into smaller, more manageable components called "shards." Each shard is responsible for processing its transactions and smart contracts, effectively allowing for parallel processing. This approach significantly boosts network capacity and reduces congestion. Ethereum, in its transition to Ethereum 2.0, has embraced sharding as a central component of its scaling strategy. The goal is to divide the Ethereum blockchain into numerous interconnected shards, with each shard processing its transactions and contracts. This architectural change enables Ethereum to handle a much larger number of transactions and applications simultaneously. Sharding introduces a fundamental shift in the way blockchain networks operate. It not only enhances scalability but also improves security and efficiency. By distributing the network's workload across multiple shards, the entire ecosystem becomes more resilient and better equipped to meet the demands of a growing user base.

In conclusion, the challenges of scalability are met with innovative solutions aimed at enhancing the performance and efficiency of blockchain networks. Layer 2 solutions like the Lightning Network and Optimistic Rollups build additional layers to process transactions, alleviating congestion on the underlying blockchain. Sharding, on the other hand, disassembles large blockchain networks into smaller, interconnected shards, introducing parallel processing and increasing network capacity. These scaling solutions are fundamental to the future of cryptocurrencies, enabling them to accommodate a global user base and further propel blockchain technology into mainstream adoption.

10.3 Predictions for the Future of Cryptocurrencies: Charting New Territories

The world of cryptocurrencies is a dynamic and rapidly evolving space. Predicting the future with absolute certainty is challenging, but certain trends and possibilities can be anticipated, providing insights into the potential directions the cryptocurrency landscape may take.

10.3.1 Mainstream Adoption: Cryptocurrencies at the Heart of Finance

One of the most significant trends in the cryptocurrency space is the move toward mainstream adoption. Over the past decade, cryptocurrencies have evolved from an obscure, experimental technology into a prominent asset class that has captured the attention of traditional financial institutions, businesses, and everyday consumers. As this trend continues, cryptocurrencies may well become an integral part of the global financial system. Leading financial institutions are beginning to offer cryptocurrency-related services, such as custody, trading, and asset management. Notable companies and payment platforms are integrating cryptocurrency payments, making digital assets more accessible for everyday transactions. The transition of Bitcoin into a legitimate asset class with institutional support is a testament to this shift.

The broader adoption of cryptocurrencies is also driven by evolving attitudes toward digital assets as viable stores of value and investment vehicles. This growing acceptance, coupled with the development of cryptocurrency infrastructure, such as decentralized exchanges and lending platforms, is further solidifying the role of cryptocurrencies in the global economy.

10.3.2   Regulation: Striking the Balance

As cryptocurrencies gain prominence, governments and regulatory bodies around the world are working to create a regulatory framework for this emerging asset class. Striking the right balance between fostering innovation and ensuring investor protection is a central challenge in this process. Regulation in the cryptocurrency space varies significantly by region and is influenced by local economic, political, and cultural factors. While some countries have embraced cryptocurrencies with open arms, others have imposed stricter measures. The regulation of cryptocurrency exchanges, anti-money laundering (AML) and know your customer (KYC) requirements, and tax policies are among the key areas where governments are focusing their attention.

The cryptocurrency community is closely watching regulatory developments, as clear legal guidelines are essential for businesses and individuals operating in this space. Effective regulation can provide stability and clarity, encouraging further adoption and investment while safeguarding against fraudulent activities and illicit finance.

10.3.3   Decentralized Finance (DeFi): Challenging the Status Quo

Decentralized Finance, or DeFi, has emerged as a groundbreaking sector within the cryptocurrency space. It represents a paradigm shift in the way financial services are conceived and delivered. By leveraging blockchain technology and smart contracts, DeFi platforms provide open and permissionless access to a wide range of financial services, including lending, borrowing, trading, and yield farming. The DeFi industry has experienced explosive growth and innovation, capturing the attention of both retail and institutional investors. These platforms challenge traditional financial institutions by offering higher yields and faster, more accessible services. In the future, DeFi may disrupt traditional banking and financial services, redefining the way individuals interact with the global financial system. However, DeFi also faces regulatory scrutiny and security challenges that require addressing. Regulatory compliance and security practices will be essential for the industry to continue its expansion while avoiding potential pitfalls.

10.3.4   Environmental Concerns: The Eco-Friendly Evolution

The environmental impact of cryptocurrency mining, particularly in the case of proof-of-work (PoW) blockchains like Bitcoin, has become a growing concern. The energy-intensive nature of PoW consensus mechanisms has led to debates about sustainability and environmental responsibility. In response to these concerns, many blockchain networks are transitioning to more energy-efficient consensus mechanisms, such as proof-of-stake (PoS) and delegated proof-of-stake (DPoS). These PoS-based networks consume significantly less energy while maintaining security and decentralization. PoS networks like Ethereum 2.0 are already in development and aim to address these environmental challenges.

As cryptocurrencies continue to gain global acceptance, the industry will need to prioritize environmentally sustainable practices. By transitioning to energy-efficient consensus mechanisms and exploring greener alternatives, the cryptocurrency community can play a part in addressing the environmental impact of blockchain technology.

10.3.5   Global Economic Impact: Redefining Financial Systems

Cryptocurrencies have the potential to significantly impact global economics in various ways. One of the most compelling prospects is providing financial services to the unbanked and underbanked populations around the world. By granting individuals access to a borderless and open financial system, cryptocurrencies can foster financial inclusion and empower individuals in underserved regions. Furthermore, cryptocurrencies have the potential to influence monetary policies, cross-border transactions, and remittances. Central banks are exploring the concept of central bank digital currencies (CBDCs), which can bridge the gap between traditional monetary systems and cryptocurrencies. These CBDCs can improve the efficiency of monetary transactions while offering enhanced financial security.

In conclusion, the future of cryptocurrencies is marked by innovation, challenges, and opportunities. Emerging technologies, such as non-fungible tokens (NFTs) and smart contracts, are shaping the industry, while scaling solutions, including Layer 2 and sharding, aim to address the scalability challenges that come with increased adoption. The cryptocurrency landscape will continue to evolve, and individuals and businesses participating in this exciting journey must remain informed, adaptable, and forward-thinking. By embracing these trends and navigating the complex dynamics of the cryptocurrency world, participants can contribute to the ongoing transformation of global finance through the power of blockchain technology. The future of cryptocurrencies is a dynamic and evolving landscape, and it promises to be a remarkable journey.

11.0 CHAPTER 11: TAXES AND REPORTING

11.1   Tax Implications of Cryptocurrency Transactions

Cryptocurrencies have introduced a new frontier of financial assets, but they also come with tax implications that users need to understand. Here are the key aspects of the tax implications of cryptocurrency transactions:

- **Capital Gains Tax:** In many countries, including the United States, cryptocurrencies are considered taxable assets, and any profits or losses resulting from their sale or exchange are subject to capital gains tax. The tax rate can vary depending on factors like the duration of the investment and the local tax laws.
- **Cryptocurrency Mining:** Mining cryptocurrency is often considered income, and miners are required to report the value of the mined coins at the time they were received. The fair market value of the mined coins may be subject to income tax.
- **Crypto-to-Crypto Transactions:** Exchanging one cryptocurrency for another can trigger a taxable event in some jurisdictions, similar to selling a cryptocurrency for fiat currency. It's essential to keep records of these transactions and report them accurately.
- **Gifts and Donations:** Giving or donating cryptocurrency can also have tax implications. Some countries provide deductions or exemptions for

charitable donations in cryptocurrency, while others may treat these transactions as gifts.

- **Staking and Yield Farming**: Earning cryptocurrency through staking or yield farming may have tax consequences. The interest or rewards received may be considered income and subject to taxation.

11.2   Reporting Requirements

Properly reporting cryptocurrency transactions is crucial to remain compliant with tax authorities. While the specific requirements can vary from one country to another, here are some general guidelines:

- **Keep Detailed Records**: Maintain comprehensive records of all cryptocurrency transactions, including dates, amounts, counterparties, and the purpose of the transaction. These records can help you calculate gains or losses accurately.
- **Use Cryptocurrency Tax Software**: Utilize specialized cryptocurrency tax software to calculate your tax liability, especially if you have a high volume of transactions. These tools can automate much of the reporting process.
- **Report Gains and Losses**: When it's time to file your taxes, accurately report any gains or losses from cryptocurrency transactions. Ensure that you're adhering to your country's tax laws and guidelines.
- **Stay Informed**: Stay informed about changing tax regulations and seek guidance from tax professionals or accountants who have experience with cryptocurrency taxation. Regulations in the cryptocurrency space are evolving, and it's essential to remain up to date.

11.3   Working with Tax Professionals

Given the complexities and changing nature of cryptocurrency taxation, working with tax professionals is a prudent step for many cryptocurrency users. Tax professionals who specialize in cryptocurrency can provide valuable assistance in navigating the tax implications of your transactions. Here's how they can help:

- **Compliance:** Tax professionals can help ensure you're in compliance with local tax laws and regulations, reducing the risk of audits, penalties, or legal issues.
- **Minimizing Tax Liability**: They can help identify legal deductions, credits, and strategies to minimize your overall tax liability.
- **Planning for the Future**: Tax professionals can provide advice on tax-efficient strategies for cryptocurrency holdings, including inheritance planning and asset protection.
- **Addressing Complex Transactions:** If you've engaged in complex cryptocurrency transactions, such as staking, yield farming, or trading on multiple exchanges, a tax professional can help navigate the associated complexities.

In summary, understanding the tax implications of your cryptocurrency transactions and meeting reporting requirements is crucial to maintain compliance and avoid potential legal issues. Given the evolving nature of cryptocurrency taxation, consulting with tax professionals who specialize in cryptocurrency can provide peace of mind and help you make informed decisions regarding your tax obligations. As we approach the concluding chapters of this guide, we will delve into the technical aspects of blockchain technology, explore advanced topics like tokenomics, and discuss the broader implications of cryptocurrencies on the global financial landscape. Stay tuned for a deeper understanding of the crypto and blockchain world.

12.0 CHAPTER 13: TOKENOMICS AND TOKEN SALES

12.1 What is Tokenomics

Tokenomics, a portmanteau of "token" and "economics," is a term used to describe the economic system and mechanics of a blockchain or cryptocurrency project. It encompasses various aspects, including the distribution, utility, and governance of tokens within the ecosystem. Understanding tokenomics is crucial for both investors and project developers.

12.2 Token Distribution

Token distribution refers to how tokens are initially created and allocated within a cryptocurrency project. Several methods of distribution exist, including:

- **Initial Coin Offerings (ICOs):** ICOs involve selling a portion of a project's tokens to early investors in exchange for capital. This was a popular method during the early days of cryptocurrency, but it has been largely replaced by other models due to regulatory concerns.
- **Security Token Offerings (STOs):** STOs are token sales that comply with securities regulations. They often represent ownership in a real-world asset and are subject to legal requirements.

- **Initial Exchange Offerings (IEOs):** IEOs are token sales conducted on cryptocurrency exchange platforms. They provide a level of trust and liquidity, but investors must use the specific exchange hosting the sale.
- **Airdrops:** In an airdrop, project tokens are distributed for free to a targeted group of individuals, often holders of a different cryptocurrency. This is a way to bootstrap a user base and create interest in the project.
- **Mining and Staking**: Some cryptocurrencies create new tokens through mining (Proof of Work) or staking (Proof of Stake) as rewards for network participation and security.

12.3   Token Utility

The utility of a cryptocurrency's tokens is a fundamental aspect of tokenomics. Tokens can serve various purposes within a blockchain ecosystem, such as:

- **Transaction Fees**: Users pay tokens as fees for processing transactions on the network.
- **Governance:** Token holders may have the right to propose and vote on changes to the blockchain's protocol and rules.
- **Access to Services:** Tokens may be used to access specific features, services, or dApps within the ecosystem.
- **Rewards:** Some tokens generate passive income through staking, earning interest, or participating in liquidity provision on decentralized exchanges.

12.4   Token Burning

Token burning is the intentional destruction of a certain number of tokens. This process reduces the total supply of tokens in circulation, potentially increasing the value of the remaining tokens. Token burning can be used as a deflationary mechanism, typically associated with cryptocurrencies like Binance Coin (BNB).

12.5   The Role of Tokenomics in Project Success

Tokenomics plays a critical role in the success and sustainability of a blockchain project. A well-designed token economy should balance the interests of investors, users, and the development team. Projects with overly complex or unfair tokenomics can face challenges with adoption and trust. Conversely, those with transparent, community-driven token economics may thrive. As we delve deeper into the complex and multifaceted world of tokenomics, it becomes clear that the economic design of a blockchain project is a foundational element, influencing everything from user behavior to project governance.

CONCLUSION: NAVIGATING THE CRYPTOCURRENCY LANDSCAPE

As we conclude this comprehensive guide to the world of cryptocurrencies and blockchain technology, it's essential to reflect on the key takeaways and encourage responsible investment and continued learning in this dynamic and innovative space.

Key Takeaways:

- **Diverse Ecosystem:** Cryptocurrencies and blockchain technology offer a vast and diverse ecosystem that goes beyond Bitcoin. Altcoins, tokens, and various applications have emerged, each with unique features and use cases.
- **Investment Strategies**: There are several investment strategies to consider, from HODLing for the long term to actively trading in the short term. Diversification and value-based investing are essential approaches.
- **Security and Risks:** Cryptocurrency investments come with risks, including market volatility, scams, and security threats. Protecting your investments with best practices like using hardware wallets and two-factor authentication is crucial.
- **Regulation and Compliance**: The regulatory landscape

for cryptocurrencies is evolving. Staying informed about the legal requirements in your region and working with tax professionals for reporting and compliance is essential.

- **Decentralized Finance (DeFi):** DeFi has introduced open and accessible financial services, but it also carries risks related to smart contracts and market volatility. Caution and due diligence are paramount.
- **Emerging Technologies**: Innovations like NFTs, smart contracts, and interoperability are reshaping the blockchain space, offering new opportunities for investment and development.
- **Scaling Solutions:** Scalability remains a challenge, but Layer 2 solutions and sharding are making strides toward improving transaction speed and cost.

Predicting the Future: The future of cryptocurrencies is marked by mainstream adoption, regulatory developments, DeFi growth, and environmental concerns. Staying adaptable is key.

Tokenomics: Understanding token distribution, utility, and governance is fundamental for both investors and project developers. Well-designed tokenomics is vital for a project's success.

Encouraging Responsible Investment and Continued Learning: Cryptocurrencies have ushered in a transformative era in finance and technology, offering opportunities and challenges in equal measure. As you navigate this landscape, here are some recommendations for responsible engagement:

Education: The cryptocurrency space is continually evolving. Commit to ongoing learning and staying informed about the latest developments, projects, and trends.

Diversification: Diversify your cryptocurrency portfolio to manage risk effectively. Conduct thorough research and due diligence when considering new investments.

Security: Prioritize the security of your investments. Use hardware wallets, enable two-factor authentication, and be cautious about sharing personal information.

Regulation: Understand the legal and tax requirements in your region related to cryptocurrency. Work with tax professionals for accurate reporting and compliance.

Risk Management: Be aware of the risks associated with cryptocurrency investments, including market volatility and security threats. Invest only what you can afford to lose.

Long-Term Perspective: While short-term trading can be enticing, consider the benefits of a long-term investment horizon, especially for cryptocurrencies with strong fundamentals.

As the world of cryptocurrencies continues to unfold, remember that responsible and informed participation is your best approach. Stay curious, stay safe, and embrace the ever-changing landscape of this exciting industry.

Thank you for joining us on this journey through the fascinating world of cryptocurrencies and blockchain technology. Whether you're a seasoned enthusiast or just starting, your exploration of this innovative field is an opportunity to shape the future of finance and technology.

Disclaimer: The information provided in this document is intended for educational and informational purposes only. It is not intended as, and shall not be considered, financial or investment advice. Cryptocurrencies and blockchain-related investments carry inherent risks, and the cryptocurrency market is known for its price volatility.

Readers are strongly advised to conduct their research, seek the counsel of qualified financial professionals, and consider their individual financial circumstances and risk tolerance before making any investment or financial decisions related to cryptocurrencies. Cryptocurrency investments are speculative and can result in substantial gains or losses. Readers should exercise caution, conduct due diligence, and consider their investment objectives. This document does not make any warranties or guarantees regarding the accuracy, completeness, or reliability of the information presented. Cryptocurrency investments are subject to regulatory changes and may have legal implications, and readers should seek legal advice when necessary.

APPENDIX

Websites:

- **CoinMarketCap:** A popular cryptocurrency market capitalization and price tracking website. (coinmarketcap.com)
- **CoinGecko:** An alternative to CoinMarketCap with additional features like DeFi data and NFT tracking. (coingecko.com)
- **CryptoSlate:** A cryptocurrency news and data platform with in-depth project profiles and industry news. (cryptoslate.com)
- **Messari:** A platform that provides crypto news, analysis, and research. (messari.io)

Crypto Wallets:

- **Ledger:** A hardware wallet for securely storing cryptocurrencies. (ledger.com)
- **Trezor:** Another popular hardware wallet for safe storage of cryptocurrencies. (trezor.io)
- **Metamask:** A popular Ethereum-based wallet for managing Ethereum and ERC-20 tokens. (metamask.io)

Exchange Platforms:

- **Binance:** A leading global cryptocurrency exchange platform for trading various digital assets. (binance.com)
- **Kraken:** A well-established exchange known for its security features and wide range of supported assets. (kraken.com)
- **Coinbase:** A user-friendly platform suitable for

beginners, offering a variety of cryptocurrencies. (coinbase.com)

Blockchain Explorers:
- **Etherscan:** A blockchain explorer for the Ethereum network, allowing you to search for transactions, addresses, and tokens. (etherscan.io)
- **Blockchair:** A blockchain search and analytics engine that supports multiple blockchains, including Bitcoin and Ethereum. (blockchair.com)

Forums and Communities:
- **BitcoinTalk:** The largest and one of the oldest forums dedicated to Bitcoin and cryptocurrency discussions. (bitcointalk.org)
- **Crypto Reddit**: Subreddits like r/Bitcoin, r/Ethereum, and r/CryptoCurrency are excellent sources for discussions, news, and updates. (reddit.com)

Educational Resources:
- **Investopedia's Cryptocurrency Section:** Investopedia provides comprehensive guides and articles on various cryptocurrency-related topics. (investopedia.com/cryptocurrency)
- **CryptoZombies:** An interactive code school that teaches you how to build blockchain apps on Ethereum. (cryptozombies.io)
- **3a16z Crypto School**: A resource by Andreessen Horowitz with lessons on cryptocurrencies and blockchain technology. (a16z.com/crypto-school)

News and Analysis:
- **The Block**: A cryptocurrency news platform providing in-depth analysis and insights. (theblockcrypto.com)
- **Decrypt:** A news and analysis platform with a focus on

cryptocurrency and blockchain. (decrypt.co)

Market Data and Analysis:
- **TradingView:** A charting platform that provides technical analysis tools for cryptocurrency and traditional markets. (tradingview.com)
- **Coin Metrics:** A provider of on-chain market and network data for multiple cryptocurrencies. (coinmetrics.io)

These resources can help cryptocurrency enthusiasts stay informed, manage their investments, and engage with the broader crypto community. Remember to conduct your due diligence and exercise caution when using new tools or services.

www.ingramcontent.com/pod-product-compliance
Lightning Source LLC
Chambersburg PA
CBHW071608270726
48661CB00019B/1651